Top 10 Worst

Ruthless Warriors

you wouldn't want to know!

Gareth Stevens
Publishing

Please visit our website, **www.garethstevens.com**. For a free color catalog of all our high-quality books, call toll free 1-800-542-2595 or fax 1-877-542-2596.

Library of Congress Cataloging-in-Publication Data

Macdonald, Fiona, 1958-
Top 10 worst ruthless warriors / Fiona Macdonald.
     p. cm. — (Top 10 worst)
Includes index.
ISBN 978-1-4339-6686-6 (pbk.)
ISBN 978-1-4339-6687-3 (6-pack)
ISBN 978-1-4339-6685-9 (library binding)
1. Soldiers—History—Juvenile literature. 2. Soldiers—Biography—Juvenile literature. 3. Military art and science—History—Juvenile literature. 4. Military history—Juvenile literature. I. Title. II. Title: Top ten worst ruthless warriors.
U51.M24 2012
355.0092'2—dc23
5939   2011018234

First Edition

Published in 2012 by
Gareth Stevens Publishing
111 East 14th Street, Suite 349
New York, NY 10003

© 2012 The Salariya Book Company Ltd

Series creator: David Salariya
Editor: Jamie Pitman
Illustrations by David Antram

Printed in Heshan, China

CPSIA compliance information: Batch #SW12GS: For further information contact Gareth Stevens, New York, New York at 1-800-542-2595.

Top **10** Worst™

Ruthless Warriors

you wouldn't want to know!

Illustrated by
David Antram

Written by
fiona Macdonald

Created & designed by
David Salariya

Contents

No mercy

Great warriors of the past appear today in films, books, and video games. Their stories may be thrilling or chilling, frightening or inspiring, but their lives show us skills, strength, and courage that many people admired and wished to copy. They may have fought at different times, with different weapons and tactics, but they all had one thing in common: they were tough, determined, and ruthless! They had no mercy!

Wellington

Britain's Duke of Wellington (1769–1852) survived 60 bloody battles in India and Europe—and defeated Napoleon (*see page 22*).

Shaka Zulu

Africa's King Shaka Zulu (around 1787–1828) created a fearsome new army—and killed anyone who disobeyed him.

Pioneered deadly new guns firing shrapnel.

Wore wellington boots (his invention).

Short spear, for fighting up close.

Rode traditional warhorse.

Bare feet, a sign of tough training.

Oxhide shield, for protection.

Power and glory

Warfare is dangerous. Soldiers get killed. So why did warriors fight so many battles? Some had no choice. They fought to defend themselves, did their duty as kings and princes, or were simply ordered to fight. Others chose to risk their lives, hoping to win power, riches, or glory. To their friends, these fighters were heroes, but their enemies hated and feared them.

Eager for empire

Here comes Hannibal, nicknamed Barca ("Lightning")! In 218 BC, he led fearsome war elephants from Carthage, North Africa, in a bid to conquer the rival empire of Rome.

What do you think this is, the circus? Move It!

Joan of Arc (1412–1431) believed that heavenly voices were telling her to fight English invaders in France.

Ihesvs Maria

Death before dishonor

At the Battle of Thermopylae in 480 BC, King Leonidas of Sparta (ancient Greece) chose to die fighting rather than to surrender.

Ruthless raiders

Viking pirates spread fear throughout Europe from AD 800 to 1100. They fought to snatch rich treasures: coins, jewels, weapons, and slaves.

I'm gonna pillage your village!

Independence!

Terrorist or freedom fighter? From 1297 to 1305, William Wallace led the Scots to fight against their English overlords.

Short but sweet

Roman gladiators' fighting skills won them fame, money—and girlfriends. But few survived to enjoy this celebrity lifestyle for long.

A world of warriors

Brave, brutal warriors have lived, fought, and died in every nation, all around the world, from the beginning of recorded history—and maybe long before.

1. *Genghis Khan*
2. *Alexander the Great*
3. *Richard I & Saladin*
4. *Napoleon*
5. *Attila the Hun*
6. *Samurai: Benkei & Yoshitsune*
7. *Julius Caesar*
8. *Hernando Cortés*
9. *Boudicca*
10. *Tipu Sultan*

8

The fame of these great warriors has survived for centuries. We know when, why, and how they fought, and which battles they won. But the names of the millions of ordinary men whom they led to fight and die have long been forgotten.

No modern warriors?

Many brave —and ruthless—men and women warriors fought in modern times. But you won't find them in this book. The wars they fought are too close to many of us. Let future histories judge them.

We shall never surrender!

9 4 5 7 2 3 1 6 10

In this book, you can read about ten of the world's most ruthless warriors—though, of course, there were many others.

№ 10

Tipu Sultan

Famed for his fierceness—and for wearing clothes striped like a tiger—Tipu Sultan fought to defend India, his homeland, from invaders. He failed (his kingdom was conquered by British armies in 1799), but won worldwide respect for his courage. "Better to live one day as a tiger than a lifetime as a sheep!" he said.

Life-size musical model of a tiger devouring a British soldier.

Vital statistics

Name: Sultan Fateh Ali Khan Shahab

Nickname: Tipu Sultan/The Tiger of Mysore

Born: India

Lived: 1750 to 1799

Career: Warrior and ruler

Fought: British troops in India, and rival Indian rulers

Died: Defending his capital city

You wouldn't want to know this:

Tipu threw prisoners into tiger pits to be killed, or so his enemies said.

Tipu had me made...

...to frighten Europeans! Owww!

Be prepared!
Always expect the very worst

fierce as a tiger

How did Tipu win his nickname? By killing a huge tiger. It sprang at him when his gun failed to fire, but Tipu fought back, armed only with a dagger.

Dinner!

Rowr!

Soldier Queen

Nature knows best

Tipu was not the only Indian warrior to fight like a tiger. War leader Shivaji (1630–1680) killed his enemies using fearsome metal blades fixed to his fingers.

Rani Lakshmibai (1835–1858) learned horse riding, archery, and self-defense. She used these skills to fight the British. She died fighting bravely alongside her men.

I call them my tiger-claws!

Swoosh

11

No 9

Boudicca

When Boudicca's husband died, he left half his kingdom to the Romans. But they demanded it all, and attacked Boudicca's family. Outraged, she led Celtic tribes to smash and burn Roman cities, sparing no one. The Romans said her troops loved to "glut themselves on the blood of their enemies."

Vital Statistics

Name:	Boudicca
Nickname:	Not known, but "Boudicca" means "Victory"
Born:	Eastern England
Lived:	Birth date unknown—died AD 61
Career:	King's wife, then (after he died) ruling queen
Fought:	Roman conquerors
Died:	Killed herself to avoid capture

You wouldn't want to know this:

Boudicca had knives fixed to her chariot's wheels, to slice up enemy soldiers.

Look out, London, here we come!

Slice

Be prepared!
Always expect the very worst

The final battle

Boudicca's brave but reckless Celtic troops were no match for trained Roman soldiers. In AD 61, in Middle England, around 80,000 Celts were stabbed to death by Roman spears. Only 400 Romans died.

> Aaaargh!

No surrender!

As Roman soldiers surrounded her chariot, Boudicca took poison and died. Her rebellion had failed, and she was too proud—and too angry—to let the Romans capture her alive.

> Yaaagh!

Another royal rebel!

Far away, in Palmyra (now Syria), another proud queen fought for independence. Zenobia (AD 240–274) kicked out Roman governors and invaded Egypt before the Romans captured her. She died in prison, and was probably beheaded.

> My stylist will be most disappointed about this!

13

N° 8

Hernando Cortés

Young, noble, but poor, Cortés was eager for adventure—and gold. In 1518, he set out to conquer the Aztec empire in Mexico—using trickery and savage punishments, such as burning captives alive. Other *conquistadors* followed him, and by 1600 most of South America was ruled by Spain.

Vital statistics

Name:	Hernando (or Hernán) Cortés
Nickname:	"Conquistador" (Conqueror)
Born:	Spain
Lived:	1485 to 1547
Career:	Soldier, explorer
Fought:	Aztecs and pirates
Died:	Of disease, back home in Spain

You wouldn't want to know this:

When Cortés landed in Mexico, he burned the ships he had arrived in. He was determined to conquer—or die trying!

Cortés tortured their emperor, and now the Aztecs are fighting back!

It's a Noche Triste (Sad Night). But we'll be back—and we'll crucify them!*

*This is how Cortés punished Aztecs who resisted him.

Be prepared!
Always expect the very worst

Holy stone

This magnificent carved stone shows a powerful Aztec prophecy: the world would end when the god Quetzalcoatl arrived from across the sea. For a while, Aztecs suspected that Cortés might be the god, and because horses were unknown in Mexico, they feared that his soldiers on horseback might be magical monsters.

Deadly diseases

The diseases spread by the conquerors, such as measles and smallpox, were even more deadly than their weapons. By around 1600, about 5 out of every 6 Aztecs had died.

Gah!

Lautaro

One Native American hero almost defeated the conquistadors. From 1553 until 1557, Lautaro led the Mapuche people of Chile to fight the Spanish invaders. They had nearly won when Lautaro was betrayed and killed.

At first the Aztecs welcomed Cortés. But he captured Aztec emperor Moctezuma, and brutally executed Aztec generals. The Aztecs fought back bravely, but their traditional weapons were powerless against European guns. By 1521, Cortés had conquered them.

No 9

Julius Caesar

Brave, ruthless, and very, very clever, Caesar was one of ancient Rome's greatest army commanders. He conquered rich nations, reformed the government, wowed crowds with his speeches, and even changed the way time was measured (we still use his calendar today). But Caesar was also frighteningly ambitious. When he took total control of Rome, his enemies killed him to set the Roman people free.

Vital Statistics

Name: Gaius Julius Caesar
Nickname: The name Caesar was used as a royal title for 2,000 years.
Born: Rome, Italy
Lived: 100 BC–44 BC
Career: Soldier and politician
Fought: To win land for Rome, and power for himself
Died: Stabbed (23 times!) by political enemies

You wouldn't want to know this:

At Caesar's victory celebrations in Rome, 2,000 war captives, 400 lions, 200 horses, 20 elephants, and many top gladiators fought and died —as entertainment.

No going back now! We're going to *rule Rome!*

After he had conquered Gaul (France and Belgium) in 49 BC, Rome's Senate (governing council) ordered Caesar to return, alone. But Caesar disobeyed, and took his army with him. With their support, he was unstoppable!

Be prepared!
Always expect the very worst

Empire adventures

While expanding his empire, Caesar claimed to fall in love with Egypt's Queen Cleopatra. Did he admire her beauty— or just want to win her kingdom?

Red = Roman Empire

BRITAIN
London
GERMANY
FRANCE
ITALY
Rome
GREECE
Black Sea
SPAIN
Mediterranean Sea
NORTH AFRICA

Wars in Gaul

No one knows how many men died fighting Caesar's troops in Gaul, but Roman historians claimed that a million tribesmen were slaughtered and that a million were captured and sold as slaves.

Where are you taking us? Have we won something?

Who dares loses...

King Vercingetorix led the Gauls to rebel against Roman rule in 42 BC. But Caesar forced him to surrender, and he was taken to Rome, paraded through the streets, then executed— horribly.

"Veni, Vidi, Vici?"

(Latin: "I came, I saw, I conquered!") Old stories say that those were Caesar's words when he invaded Britain in 55–54 BC. In fact, Caesar never said them—and he failed to conquer Britain. But these old stories tell us what people thought about his proud, confident character.

Retreat!

№ 6

Samurai

Vital Statistics ~ Benkei

Name: Saitō Musashibō Benkei
Nickname: Benkei
Born: Japan
Lived: 1155 to 1189
Career: Warrior monk
Fought: Alongside famous Samurai (noble warrior) Yoshitsune

You wouldn't want to know this:

Benkei was said to be a "demon child," with sharp pointed teeth and long hair. He grew up to be over 6 1/2 feet (2 m) tall!

Warrior monk Benkei hoped to make a magic sword from the tips of 1,000 others. So he prowled along Gojo Bridge, fighting any samurai who dared to cross it. He killed 999 warriors and took their weapons, but then the young soldier Yoshitsune defeated him. The two became comrades for the rest of their lives, fighting—and dying—together.

He's too quick! I can't catch him, even with my *naginata!**

Grr!

* killer blade fixed to a long pole

Be prepared!
Always expect the very worst

Charge!

Wet, wet, wet

In 1184, enemies destroyed the only bridge over which Yoshitsune and Benkei could escape to safety after a battle. With amazing courage, they rode into the raging river—and survived to reach the other side.

I hope I don't lose my shoes...

What a way to go!

Shot full of enemy arrows while defending a castle, Benkei died on his feet, fighting bravely. Strangely, his body stayed standing for many hours afterwards. No one dared approach it.

Vital statistics ~ Yoshitsune

Name: Minamoto no Yoshitsune

Nickname: Ushiwaka-maru ("young ox")

Born: Japan

Lived: 1159 to 1189

Career: The most famous warrior of his age

Died: Killed himself to avoid the shame of defeat

You wouldn't want to know this:

After Yoshitsune died, his head was cut off, pickled in *sake* (Japanese rice wine) and sent to the leader of his enemies.

One more way to frighten the enemy! They'll think I'm a ghost!

19

No 5

Attila the Hun

"The Terror of all Europe!"
For fifteen frightful
years, warlord Attila
led Hun tribes to
attack and destroy. The
Huns swept away what
peaceful citizens valued most
—towns, churches, art, sports,
music, farms, workshops,
markets, family life, and the
chance to earn a living.
But the Huns got what
they came to find—land,
loot, and money.

Vital statistics

Name: Attila ("father of his people")

Nickname: Scourge (Punishment) of God

Born: Hungary

Lived: AD 406–453

Career: Overlord of nomad tribes, known as "Huns"

Fought: Europe, Central Asia

Died: In bed, on his wedding night, from a nosebleed

You wouldn't want to know this:

At first, Attila shared power with his brother. But then he killed him, so that he could rule alone.

We've come to punish... and rob... and kill you!

20

Be prepared!
Always expect the very worst

Destroyers!

In AD 435, Attila and his Huns attacked eastern Europe, spreading death and destruction. They wrecked 70 great cities, looting churches full of holy treasures and massacring priests, monks, and nuns.

The Huns defeated Roman armies close to the Roman city of Constantinople (now Istanbul) in AD 443. The Romans paid Attila over 2 tons of gold to go away, but he wanted more...

Fighting for food

From AD 451–452, Attila led his Huns westward, towards Rome. His army destroyed all farm crops and livestock so that the Romans would starve. But when the Huns also ran short of food, Attila retreated, and died, unexpectedly, in bed.

No 4

Napoleon

Vital Statistics

Name: Napoleon Bonaparte
Nickname: "Boney"
Born: Corsica (an island in the Mediterranean Sea)
1769 to 1821
Lived:
Career: Army commander; Emperor of France
Fought: To conquer all of Europe—and beyond
Died: In prison, from illness or maybe accidental poisoning

You wouldn't want to know this:

Napoleon's enemies claimed that he ate naughty children!

Genius or madman? No one could be sure! From humble beginnings, Napoleon used ruthless warrior skills and supreme self-confidence to become emperor of France. He won many famous victories, but he did not know when to stop fighting. His wars almost bankrupted France, and killed six million French and enemy soldiers.

One day glory, the next, disaster...

We're dying of cold and hunger! Curse you!

Be prepared!
Always expect the very worst

There is no such word as 'impossible'!

Breaking the rules

Napoleon became famous for his courage and daring. He won many battles using risky shortcuts and surprise maneuvers. When invading Italy in 1796, he told his troops to "move quickly and be ruthless about it."

Napoleon's Empire

Look out! Enemy approaching!

The french advantage

Napoleon's troops were better organized and more highly trained than any previous French army. They also had more accurate cannons and swift horse-drawn gun carriages to rush them into battle. They even used hot air balloons for spying.

Between 1799 and 1814, Napoleon won control of Europe. But after he was defeated by Britain and its allies at the Battle of Waterloo (1815), French power collapsed quickly.

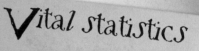

 No 3

Richard I & Saladin

Vital statistics

Name: Salah al-Din ibn Ayyub
Nickname: Saladin
Born: Iraq
Lived: 1138 to 1193
Career: Sultan (ruler)
Fought: To capture Jerusalem. Succeeded in 1187.
Died: Of fever, in Syria

Richard the Lionheart and Saladin—one Christian, one Muslim. These two warriors each believed that they were fighting for God. They led rival armies during the Third Crusade—a war between European and Middle Eastern powers for the holy city of Jerusalem. Richard and Saladin never met face to face, but they admired each other's courage and fighting skills.

You wouldn't want to know this:

Saladin was famously merciful, but he did kill top Christian knights, his most dangerous enemies.

A clever way to kill

In 1187, at the Battle of Hattin, Saladin set fire to the dry grass and bushes around a marching Crusader army, which dazed and confused them. The next day they were no match for Saladin's soldiers. Over 10,000 Crusaders were killed.

24

It is not the custom of kings to kill kings.

Be prepared!
Always expect the very worst

Vital Statistics

Name: Richard I/Richard Plantagenet
Nickname: The Lionheart
Born: England
Lived: 1157 to 1199
Career: King of England
Fought: To defeat Saladin in the Holy Land. Succeeded in 1191.
Died: Shot by a sniper at a French castle.

You wouldn't want to know this:

Richard ruled lands in France so ruthlessly that the people there rebelled against him.

Cash for a Crusade

To pay for his army, Richard made the English pay heavy, unfair taxes, nicknamed the "Saladin Tithe," and sold top government jobs to anyone who would pay. He even said, "I will sell London if I can find a buyer."

Ching!

Rough justice

Saladin was often merciful, but he could also be ruthless. In 1187, he captured Raynald of Châtillon—a very nasty character who attacked peaceful merchants, religious pilgrims, and farmers. Although Raynald begged for his life, Saladin beheaded him.

After capturing the city of Acre in 1191, Richard had nearly 3,000 Muslim hostages killed—even though he had promised them safety. Why so ruthless? He couldn't take them into battle—and dared not risk leaving them behind.

I want to make the whole world tremble!

No 2

Alexander the Great

Small, stout, strong-willed, and hot-tempered but utterly charming, Alexander's personality and ruthless ambition made him the greatest army commander. Who else could have persuaded troops to follow him "to the ends of the earth"? He relied on cleverness and careful planning—not brute force—to win, and he never lost a battle!

Alexander was born with a twisted neck, so he was always gazing upwards.

Vital Statistics

Name: Alexander III
Nickname: The Great
Born: Macedonia
Lived: 356 to 323 BC
Career: King of Macedonia; army commander
Fought: To conquer the world
Died: In Babylon (Iraq), perhaps poisoned

You wouldn't want to know this:

In a fury, Alexander set fire to the magnificent capital city of the mighty Persian empire (now Iran and the nearby lands). It was completely destroyed.

A god among men – that's me!

After conquering Egypt in 332 BC, Alexander visited the temple of Amun, the sun god. There, an oracle declared him the "son of the god," "master of the universe," and also pharaoh of Egypt.

Be prepared!
Always expect the very worst

At just 13 years old, Alexander tamed a mighty warhorse, Bucephalus. He saw that the horse was frightened by its own shadow, and gently turned it to face the sun.

To the ends of the earth

MACEDONIA
GREECE
Black Sea
Gordion
Caspian Sea
SOGDIANA
BACTRIA
Tyre
SYRIA
MESOPOTAMIA
Babylon
PERSIA
Persepolis
INDIA
Alexandria
BABYLONIA
Persian Gulf
Indian Ocean
EGYPT
Red Sea

Knotty problem

When Alexander visited Gordion in 333 BC, he saw an ancient knot that no one could untie—and sliced straight through it! A prophecy said that the first man to free the knot would become king of Asia.

Chop

After conquering Greece, the Balkans, and Egypt, Alexander's army headed east into unknown, hostile territory. He overpowered the splendid Persian Empire, together with many smaller kingdoms, until his troops reached India.

Final frontier

Alexander was not all-powerful. When he reached the River Hyphasis in India, the water was deep and fast-flowing, and Indian armies with fierce war elephants waited on the other side. His men turned back, refusing to go further.

Glark!

What's that?! A monster?!

Hrrrrrmmmphh!

No 1

Genghis Khan

While he lived, and for centuries after, Genghis Khan was probably the most feared man on Earth. He was certainly its most ruthless destroyer—over 40 million men, women, and children were killed by his armies. But Genghis was also the first to unite and organize the Mongol tribes of Central Asia, and he led them to conquer the largest empire the world had ever seen.

> This tower of enemy skulls celebrates Genghis Khan's latest victory. See how great he is!

Vital Statistics

Name: Borjigin Temujin
Nickname: Genghis Khan ("True Ruler" or "Ruler of All")
Born: Mongolia
Lived: 1162 to 1227
Career: Uniting Mongol tribes; conquering a vast empire
Fought: To win more land
Died: A mystery!

You wouldn't want to know this:

Genghis Khan's body was carried back to his homeland. Every living creature that it passed was killed, to go with him to the world of the dead.

Be prepared!
Always expect the very worst

If anyone can, Genghis Khan!

Hit and run

Mongol warriors fought on horseback, galloping up to enemies and firing arrows. They beseiged cities with giant catapults and battering rams. If the citizens surrendered and paid a ransom, they were usually allowed to live— in fear of the next Mongol attack!

Serves them right?!

Anyone who dared oppose Genghis Khan was cruelly punished. He murdered one enemy leader by pouring molten metal into his eyes and ears. Others were crushed to death.

So that's what heavy metal sounds like!

Timur

Genghis Khan had many wives and children, and we can still trace his descendants today. One was Timur Lenk (1336–1405), an ambitious ruler of Central Asia who was chosen to lead after winning a hat-throwing game that tested his aiming skills. He died trying to conquer China.

fwoosh!

Genghis Khan's Empire

Awesome empire

In just 21 years, from 1206 to 1227, Genghis Khan took control of lands stretching from the Pacific Ocean to the Caspian Sea. His conquests created new laws, nations, ways of writing, the first banknotes, and— through terror of Mongol punishments—long-lasting peace.

29

Glossary

Aztecs An ancient civilization, powerful in central Mexico in the 14th and 15th centuries AD.

Balkans A region in southeastern Europe between Greece and Hungary.

Bankrupt Having no money.

Beseige To surround a castle, town, or village so people cannot get in or out.

Celts Peoples who shared a culture and a group of languages. They flourished in Europe between around 800 BC and AD 100.

Comrades People who fight together on the same side.

Conquest The act of conquering. The efforts made by an army and its commanders to conquer a place.

Crusades A series of wars led by European rulers between around AD 1096 and AD 1500. They aimed to capture land in the Middle East (the "Holy Land"), around the city of Jerusalem.

Descendant A child, grandchild, great-grandchild, great-great-grandchild, and so on, of a person.

Gaul A large area of ancient Europe, inhabited mostly by Celtic tribes. In Caesar's time, it included France, Belgium, Luxembourg, and part of south Germany.

Governor An official or politician who rules on behalf of a king or government.

Hostages People held against their will whose captors want to exchange their lives for a ransom, which is often a large sum of money.

Huns Nomad tribes from Central Asia. Around AD 400, they conquered vast areas of land in Europe.

Livestock Animals raised specifically to provide people with labor, food, or fur.

Looting Stealing from places that have been damaged by natural disasters or war.

30

Maneuvers The planned movements of an army.

Measles A viral infection that causes a rash, inflammation and, in the past, death. Today it can be prevented by vaccination.

Mongols Nomad tribes based in Mongolia. In the 13th and 14th centuries AD, they conquered the largest empire the world had ever seen. It stretched from China to eastern Europe.

Oracle In ancient history, a person who was said to speak for the gods, often predicting the future.

Pharaoh The name given to the king of ancient Egypt. It means "Great House."

Pillage To steal from a place that is under attack.

Prophecy A prediction of the future.

Samurai A professional and highly respected Japanese warrior.

Senate In ancient Rome, the assembly of people who made decisions on behalf of the public.

Shrapnel A small, sharp piece of metal from a larger metal object, such as a shell, which has exploded.

Smallpox A dangerous infectious disease, caused by a virus.

Sniper A soldier with very accurate aim who can shoot at, and hit, enemies from a distance.

Terrorist Someone who uses violence and fear to get what they want.

Index

32